NOT EVERYONE IS GOING TO LIKE YOU

Thoughts from a Former People Pleaser

Rinny Perkins

Kokila

For Meme
—R.P.

Kokila
An imprint of Penguin Random House LLC, New York

First published in the United States of America by Kokila,
an imprint of Penguin Random House LLC, 2023

Copyright © 2023 by Rinny Perkins

Visit us online at penguinrandomhouse.com.

Library of Congress Cataloging-in-Publication Data is available.

Manufactured in China

ISBN 9780593325520

10 9 8 7 6 5 4 3 2 1
TOPL

This book was edited by Sydnee Monday, copy edited by Ariela Rudy Zaltzman, and designed by Jasmin Rubero. The production was supervised by Tabitha Dulla and Cherisse Landau.
Text set in Acrom Family

This is a work of nonfiction. Some names and identifying details have been changed.

The publisher does not have any control over and does not assume any responsibility for author or third-party websites or their content.

Table of Contents

CHAPTER 1

Who?
What?
Why?

WHY DO ALL THE BLACK GIRLS GET IN TROUBLE FOR TALKING?

Why Do the Black Girls Get In Trouble for Talking?

It started in elementary school. I was constantly reprimanded for "talking too much," and put in various corners of the classroom, away from other students, to prevent conversations about Nickelodeon.

In the fifth grade, my entire desk group of four kids was prohibited from participating in a class activity because of talking. When I reached middle school, I was given in-school suspension for making a newsletter about a class trip to Disneyland, which I handed out to my classmates before first period.

In the seventh grade, I was put out of my typing class for talking. I was given demerits. I received poor marks on progress reports.

Sure, overhearing a conversation about cartoons and who left a note under their crush's desk (me) can be distracting during lessons. However, most of the time, a few other students and I were admonished for talking when the class was in between activities and new work had yet to be assigned.

Black girls have always been pushed to be seen and not heard, to not make too much noise or rock the boat to avoid conflict or the discomfort of others.

So if I spent a healthy chunk of my formative years relegated to a desk in the corner of a classroom because I was talking about the Spice Girls, it's no wonder I also spent almost a decade trying to figure out how in the hell I'm supposed to affirm myself.

MICROAGGRESSION BINGO

"IS THAT YOUR REAL HAIR?"	"I'M JUST NOT ATTRACTED TO BLACK GIRLS"	"YOU'RE TOO AGGRESSIVE"	PERSONAL SPACE IGNORED BY A STRANGER	UNDERPAID
"I'M ALMOST AS DARK AS YOU"	"YOUR TONE IS REALLY INTIMIDATING"	"YOU'RE ONLY HERE BECAUSE OF AFFIRMATIVE ACTION"	"YOU'RE PRETTY FOR A DARK-SKIN GIRL"	"YOUR HAIR IS DISTRACTING"
"THAT'S SO GHETTO"	BEING FOLLOWED WHILE SHOPPING	"CAN I TOUCH YOUR HAIR?"	OVERLOOKED AT WORK	"YOU'RE SO ARTICULATE"
"YOU'RE INTIMIDATING"	WAITED DECADES FOR COSMETICS THAT MATCH YOUR SKIN TONE	SOMEONE ASSUMED THAT YOU SPEAK FOR ALL BLACK PEOPLE	CONCERNS ON RACE DISMISSED	"I DON'T SEE COLOR"
OVERLOOKED AT SCHOOL	NOT GIVEN SPACE TO SPEAK	"YOU'RE ONE OF THE GOOD ONES"	ONLY SPEAKS TO YOU IN AAVE BUT IS NOT BLACK	REFUSES TO PRONOUNCE YOUR NAME CORRECTLY

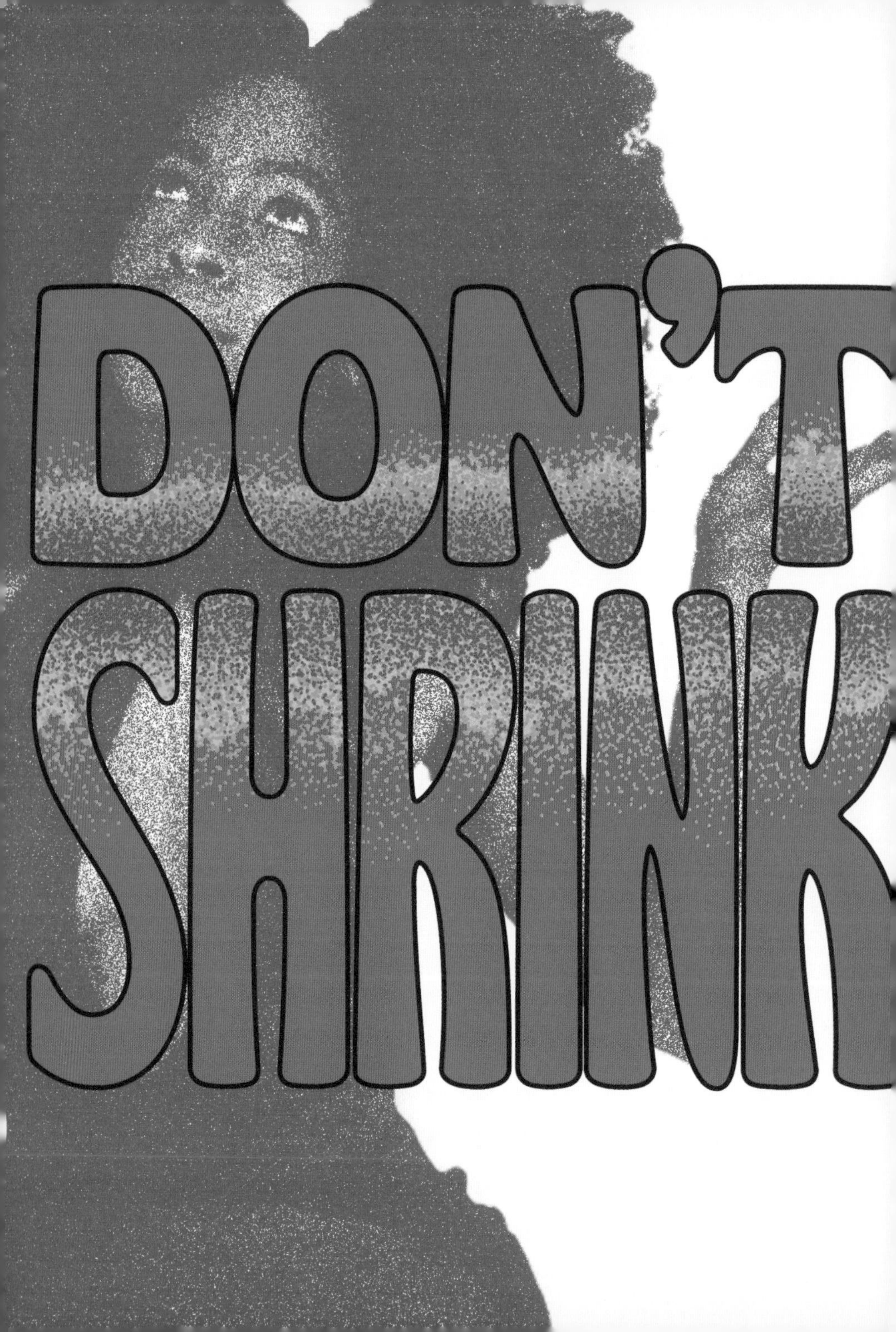
DON'T
SHRINK

I Will Not Shrink Myself for You

The cheat code to leveling up is refusing to shrink yourself.

Am I too aggressive?
Am I feeding into a stereotype?
Is my wholeness palatable enough to be consumed?

You might be tempted to fit into a box.

You might try to monitor the way you talk.

You might try to hide your hair texture in styles considered "tame" or whatever that bullshit-ass coworker of yours said.

You might avoid voicing your thoughts because you want to be seen as a "team player."

Shrinking is not an option, sis. The concept of shrinking yourself allows only for temporary "acceptance."

This isn't real acceptance.

Eventually, you will get tired of making yourself smaller in hopes that someone might "tolerate" your identity.

Take up space.

Don't hold back.

ANGELA BASSETT DESERVED AN OSCAR FOR *WAITING TO EXHALE* IN 1995.

The pageantry of life as a Black woman is consistently working three times harder to win a crown only to have your talent ignored.

And you are never considered for the title of Miss Congeniality.

BEYONCÉ DESERVED THE ALBUM OF THE YEAR GRAMMY FOR *LEMONADE.*

YOU DON'T HAVE TO BE CHILL

YOUR EXISTENCE IS NOT VALIDATED BY ANYONE'S DUSTY-ASS OPINION

Prioritize Yourself
Make choices based on your own personal needs.
Stop ignoring your intuition. It's there for a motherfuckin'
reason, sis.

Black Girl Club

A couple years ago, I dated a clown who ended up treating me like I was disposable. I could sense they were pulling away, and I wanted to keep it 100, so being the Aries I am, I brought attention to their dwindling engagement and slow responses to my texts. I was prepared to have this conversation, and then we could both go our separate ways.

They insisted everything was fine and that they wanted to continue seeing me. We had this conversation a minimum of three times because their behavior wasn't matching their words. In spite of it all, I continued to oblige in an attempt to trust their word and not my intuition. Fast-forward: It's a holiday weekend and my former lukewarm lover is making out with another woman in front of me at an outdoor movie screening.

I felt lower than low. After learning that someone you dated for almost six months doesn't even respect you enough to avoid causing you unnecessary pain, you can't help but feel disposable. Dating in LA as a Black woman, for me, always had this gross undertone of low desirability. That then translated to not being respected enough to receive transparency, even when I asked for it. This had been the norm of my dating life for almost three years.

I felt like my feelings didn't matter. I felt like I wasn't enough, and at my lowest, I felt like I never would be.

After that experience, I wanted to reclaim my power and restore confidence in my identity as a Black woman. I wanted to take up space. I wanted folks to know, "I'm in this bitch!" so I made these Black Girl Club jackets to let folks know this was something for us that you can't pay to get into, something to uplift Black girls through all the bullshit. A dating study* citing Black women as the "least desirable" cannot erase our significance.

*2010 OkCupid Study

AM I INVISIBLE?
AM I INVISIBLE?
AM I INVISIBLE?
AM I INVISIBLE?
AM I INVISIBLE?
AM I INVISIBLE?
AM I INVISIBLE?
AM I INVISIBLE?
AM I INVISIBLE?
AM I INVISIBLE?
AM I INVISIBLE?
AM I INVISIBLE?
AM I INVISIBLE?

IMPORTAN

FOR

FROM

MESSAGE Y'all will disrespect and degrade Black women and then isolate them and invalidate their feelings by labeling them as "angry Black women." Y'all tear down and make fun of Black women without any regard for them. Being the only Black woman in a group of Non-Black women and dealing with the microaggressions of being isolated from a group and labeled an "angry Black woman" after a clear transgression is something that never goes away.

Black women's pain is constantly minimized and disregarded. Y'all don't value Black women's presence. Y'all don't value Black women's relationships/friendships with you unless you can benefit. To the Black girls experiencing this, I'm so sorry. It happens at work. It happens within friend groups. No one advocates for Black women except Black women. There is a reason why "misogynoir" is clearly labeled outside of plain ol' "misogyny." Y'all laugh at the expense of Black girls. Y'all don't protect Black girls. I'm fucking tired and over this shit. And if it applies to you, it APPLIES.

In college, I was the only Black person in my English course and I'd formed a friendship with the only other POC in class. Once during group activity, he took it upon himself to refer to me as a "nigga" in front of the other white students we were grouped with, something he hadn't done before. When I voiced how offensive and inappropriate it was, all of a sudden I didn't have a friend in class anymore.

MESSAGE

These microaggressions followed me at work. Non-Black coworkers would interpret my communication style as "aggressive." As an adult, it manifests when I'm in a group of non-Black women and constantly have to justify and validate my own feelings. To be vulnerable enough to voice someone hurting your feelings as a Black woman subjects you to being attacked. You're instantly in the wrong. You experience it with partners. The amount of times I've been viewed as disposable by partners who violated me or my body and invalidated my right to safety is outright insulting. I was socialized to be the bigger person or not react/voice my opinion of mistreatment for fear of being the angry Black girl they were dating. News flash: They're already treating you as if you're beneath them by insinuating you're disposable. Might as well let them have it. Black women should not have to tirelessly explain that you hurt their feelings for you to still not listen. How many times have you stood there and explained to someone the misogynoir in what they've done and STILL feel like you weren't heard? It's as if they listened to what you said but still didn't apply it to their behavior, because at their core, they don't believe they're wrong. I have exited spaces that have made me feel othered/ostracized.

Black women are not overreacting. Black women are not dragging shit on when they speak up for themselves. You dehumanize us and only affiliate and boost us up when you see us doing good to feel better about yourself. We're forced to be the bigger person unless we want to face being further ostracized. Black women are denied grace and the fortitude of softness, and it's fucking gross.

Call me back.

OVERWORKED
OVERLOOKED
UNDERREPRESENTED

Knowing Your Value
Goes Harder

Knowing your value goes harder than doing a bunch of labor to convince someone of your value.

For the longest time, I suffered from the wack train of thought that in order for someone to want to hang out with you or even remotely be happy to know you, you needed to have immense social currency. You needed to be objectively successful. Basically, you needed "clout."

Surely, if you're on a well-known TV show or included in some major publication's 30 under 30 list, no one will treat you like shit. That assumption is 1000 percent wrong. Yes, there are some people who want to use their proximity to you, and some people will just want to flat-out use you to their benefit.

None of that translates to your own personal value, and none of that means that they won't treat you like you don't matter at the drop of a hat.

If you have to work just as hard to keep a friend group interested in you as you would to build up a career, it's best to let it fall by the wayside.

PERFECTION IS A WASTE OF TIME

WERE YOU UNDER THE IMPRESSION THAT I VALUED YOUR OPINION ON MY BODY?

THERE'S NOTHING WRONG WITH TAKING UP SPACE AND ADVOCATING FOR YOURSELF

CHAPTER 2

Mentally Prepared

'SCUSE ME

WHY HAVEN'T YOU BEEN TO THERAPY?

- ☐ *My family says I just need to pray about it*
- ☐ *People will think something is wrong with me*
- ☐ *I'm afraid there really is something wrong with me*
- ☐ *No money/insurance*
- ☐ *I can just talk about it in the group chat*
- ☐ *I can just talk to my partner about my problems*
- ☐ *Everything will blow over*

Relax, Relate, Release

The first time I went to therapy, I was around the age of six or seven. My parents divorced when I was a year old, and my dad didn't even live in the same city as me. I didn't think going to therapy was a big deal then, because let's face it, I was a kid who got to sit around and play with toys for an hour while a therapist tried to coax me into talking about my feelings. Spoiler alert: I was only there for the toys. To this day, I'm not clear on why my mom thought I needed to see a therapist then. I never had any trouble in school outside of talking too much.

It wasn't until I was about eleven or twelve that I went to therapy again. Naturally, by this time, the stigma associated with going to see a mental health professional rubbed off on me. I was convinced it wasn't for people like me. It was for kids with "real problems," the ones who would get in-school suspension for setting off stink bombs in the hallways or talking back to teachers. It wasn't for me! I was a cheerleader! I was on the honor roll! I got the role of Aunt in the school's production of *Cinderella* (when I should've been cast as the lead, but that's another story). I wasn't a problem child, so I didn't need therapy. The lie detector determined that was a lie. I'd ask my mom why she was sending me to therapy. "Do you think there's something wrong with me?" She just dropped me off and picked me up as if it was a piano lesson that she was never involved in. Because of this, I was admittedly resentful and defiant throughout those sessions in my adolescence. Which brings me to my point: Just because you think you're one of the "regular girls" who listened to Ashanti and Panic! at the Disco and enjoyed eating pizza and maintained perfect attendance in school doesn't mean you can't benefit from therapy. Regular girls go to therapy, sis.

I first went to therapy of my own accord around 2011 after a breakup that brought on my first dance with depression. Naturally, I thought I could just get through it on my own, but it had been months and I still hadn't gotten through it. I had zero appetite. I couldn't sleep, and I woke up every night at 3 am. I needed help. I was lucky enough to have health insurance at the time, so I began researching online and I found a Black psychologist that was near my school who I could see.

Fourth Time's a Charm

In 2016, I quit a job that gave me so much anxiety, I couldn't even sleep at night. I was constantly worried I would lose everything since everything depended on my boss's mood, which tended to fluctuate a lot (I was fired and hired twice in one month). But what about money? This time, I was no longer on my parent's insurance, but fortunately there are counseling centers that offer low-cost and sliding scale sessions. I found a local counseling center in LA that offered a sliding scale program. Because of the income-based fee schedule, I was able to see a therapist weekly for a couple years for no more than $13 a session. The downside was the waiting list was about six weeks long, and I didn't get to choose my therapist. However, I lucked out and got one that worked for me until I found someone new with the insurance I eventually secured.

Therapy has given me the tools to establish boundaries and unpack the traumas that I would've otherwise overlooked on my personal journey to self-healing.

I Mean Fifth Time's a Charm

Today, I regularly go to therapy. I'm blessed to have insurance provided through my union. I started sessions when I was stuck in a cycle of a toxic relationship and roommate situation that drained almost every bit of my being. I am now in a place where I feel more assertive in myself. I'm prioritizing my goals. I'm not procrasti– Let me stop lying. (I'm still working on that last one.) I'm recognizing the value I have as a Black woman, even when we're constantly shitted on in a society that barely recognizes our humanity.

Now I'm definitely a "DAMN, I KNOW YOU SEE ME" kind of bitch when it comes to taking up space, instead of hoping others see me and maybe consider giving me a teaspoon of respect. Therapy saved me.

Reduced and Reused

It wasn't until maybe two years ago that I recognized the root cause of my people pleasing stemmed from abandonment issues that I developed as a kid. Surely, if others saw how much I needlessly sacrificed at any given minute, no one would assume I was worth leaving behind.

I coped with abandonment in childhood by seeking hyperindependence. I held two jobs at sixteen to cover the cost of driver's ed and my license, since my grandma's house was a two-hour bus ride from school. I figured out early that the path of least resistance was the one where I depended on myself, so I sought out opportunities to make sure I had as much control of my life as possible.

I've coped with feelings of abandonment as an adult by overextending myself in unbalanced relationships, attempting to keep emotional distance, more hyperindependence, and hypercriticism masked as perfectionism.

Hypercriticism is the one trait that I still struggle most with. In situations where I've been wrong, no matter how small, the hypercriticism will immediately go into overdrive and validate every other negative thing I believe about myself. It wasn't until my therapist pointed out this punitive-ass behavior that I finally understood there's a difference between holding yourself accountable for your actions and berating yourself for your mistakes.

PILLS
PILLS
PILLS

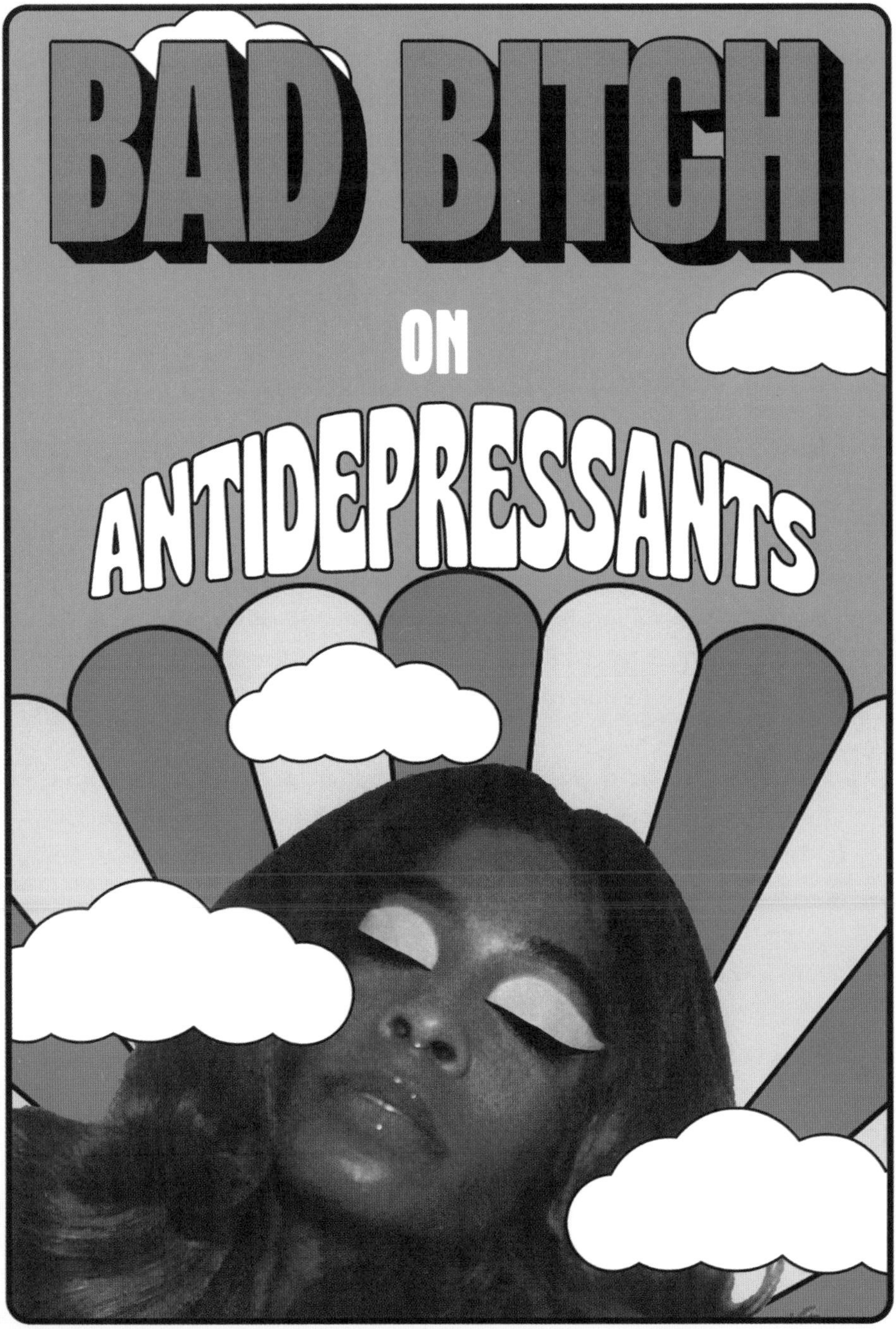
BAD BITCH
ON
ANTIDEPRESSANTS

Bad Bitch on Antidepressants

In February 2019, I started antidepressants.

    Freeze frame Yep, that's me. I bet you're wondering how I got here. It all began when . . .

    I started noticing something was incredibly off. Sure, I had been depressed for a stint or two in the past, but this time was different. I felt weighed down and suffocated. I felt as if I couldn't escape this feeling of distress. It was more than just feeling sad.

    At 10 am on a Saturday morning, after a successful art show the previous night, I bought a $30 train ticket from LA to Santa Barbara on a whim. I needed to get away. I needed space. I had a partner at the time who contributed to this suffocation by refusing to give me the space I needed, and my living situation was a bit of a nightmare. I texted my therapist that I was contemplating this random trip, and she agreed that I should take some time away.

    I stayed for one night and felt a bit lighter, but as soon as I came back to LA, I felt the clouds return. I cried. I couldn't do this anymore. I desperately looked to find a psychiatrist who was accepting patients and my insurance. This proved to be harder than finding a one-bedroom apartment for under $1,000 a month in New York City.

I finally had my initial appointment with a psychiatrist, who started me on a low dose of antidepressants. I thought my problems were pretty much solved . . . Oh, but I was wrong.

My Antidepressant Journey

Day 1: Started my prescription for Prozac, things are looking up.

Day 5: Linkin Park-Numb.mp3

Day 6: Damn, I have no desire for sex at all.

Day 7: Why is it so hard to orgasm?

Day 8: *after realizing I can't orgasm with ease* I gotta get off this shit.

I do my own research into SSRIs, or Selective Serotonin Reuptake Inhibitors (something I should've done prior to accepting any prescription), and I discover that a lot of them, including Prozac, decrease your libido dramatically. For someone like me, that's a hard pass.

I then look into NDRIs, or norepinephrine–dopamine reuptake inhibitors, such as Wellbutrin, which have been known to not inhibit you from orgasming and in some cases even boost libido. I had my psychiatrist switch me to Wellbutrin XL 150 mg post-haste and haven't looked back since.

ADHD: A Love Story

Sometime in 2017, I started to recognize symptoms of ADHD in myself. My therapist suggested I see a psychiatrist, so I went. During the 30-minute visit, I explained what I'd been experiencing, and she prescribed 10 mg of Adderall. After jumping through hoops with multiple pharmacies, I was finally able to get my prescription filled. I took one tablet, which I presumed was the appropriate dose given the label that read "Take one tablet twice a day." Within 20 minutes, I felt symptoms of intense anxiety. My heart was racing even though I was sitting completely still.

I contacted my psychiatrist, who then told me she'd only prescribed half of the 10 mg dose.

[blank stare]

Now, I'm not sure if it was the ADHD symptoms (lack of focus, failure to pay attention to detail) that made me miss that important note during the appointment, or if she was mistaken and didn't inform me of this. After all, the bottle did say, "Take one tablet twice a day."

After that first attempt, I decided to give up on the medication altogether and let my ADHD go untreated for almost five years. It wasn't until sometime between 2020 and 2022 that the symptoms began to manifest on a much larger scale, to the point where I could no longer overlook what was happening.

I mistakenly thought I was just burnt out for the longest time because I was writing a book and a pilot, acting, running a store, and designing large-scale campaigns for big companies. Surely, I thought to myself, I was just overworked. However, when I got to the point where I struggled to produce in the way I was used to, I knew I had to do something different. I brought it up again to my therapist, who at the time didn't do much to validate my symptoms.

In our sessions, the therapist would say things like, "You just need to get better organized," "You need a new system to practice better habits," "You need a planner," all the while knowing that I was on my sixth Passion Planner® and most of the previously color-coded pages were now empty. Even though I knew she was wrong (yes, healthcare providers can indeed be wrong), I began to internalize her doubt in my previous diagnosis and didn't prioritize seeking additional help. I thought if someone who knew the DSM (Diagnostic and Statistical Manual of Mental Disorders) didn't believe me enough to advocate looking into it any further, it was something else.

Later, I came across a few articles online by Black women who were diagnosed with ADHD. For the first time in a while, I began to feel both validated and empowered to push myself to seek more help. I'm now seeing a new psychiatrist that listens and validates my concerns. During my ADHD evaluation, she even provided me with an evaluation form that specified how ADHD symptoms show up differently in women because previous studies have limited research to cis men. I'm now managing these symptoms with a new medication that doesn't send my anxiety into overdrive. Remember, there's no one-size-fits-all approach to mental healthcare. While it's important to advocate for yourself and find a provider who will validate your concerns, I also understand it's exhausting and even a privilege to go so long without treatment to find the right fit. On top of it all, Black women have historically had our symptoms dismissed within the healthcare system. We are often underdiagnosed and underprescribed by healthcare providers. Thankfully, over the past few years, multiple organizations with a core focus on intersectionality in healthcare have advocated for accessibility.

SEX IS GREAT, BUT HAVE YOU EVER HAD A HEALTHCARE PROVIDER VALIDATE YOUR CONCERNS?

Stay Out of My Business

While I was completely content with being on anti-depressants and feeling like I could function, my joy wasn't exactly readily accepted by certain people in my life:

- My ex who claimed I needed to learn how to "be happy without those pills" and that I should just try *insert dumb-ass suggestion*
- My friend who needed to be in therapy his damn self, but thought somehow antidepressants made me weak?

If you've gotten to the point where you've sought out the antidepressant route, please don't let clowns who don't know their asshole from their mouth deter you. You are still a bad bitch and there ain't no shame in prioritizing your mental health.

DON'T LET ANYONE SHAME YOU FROM GETTING HELP

COME AND GO AS YOU PLEASE

It's okay!

You can leave a therapist if it's not working out

Can We Bring This to a Formal Close?

Yes, we're in therapy to work on ourselves. However, it's equally important that we listen to ourselves in the process. While therapy can be uncomfortable, you have space to ensure your needs are being met. If you feel like your therapist isn't receptive to feedback, maybe you should bounce. You don't have to stick with the first therapist you see just because. A healthy relationship with a therapist is possible. If one doesn't work out, try another. If you've been seeing a therapist for a while and at any point you begin to feel the sessions have become increasingly counterproductive, you are well within your right to switch to another mental health provider.

I was seeing a therapist for almost two years, and as we neared the two-year mark, she began to consistently cancel and reschedule appointments. It started out with a few missed sessions here and there, and then it ramped up to an almost weekly basis. Initially, I had the flexibility in my schedule to adjust to these requests, but there came a time when I needed more stability and support, and she just wasn't available. I would constantly question if I was being too needy of a client or if my needs truly weren't being met. After all, I broached the topic of availability to her a few months prior and she just brushed me off. Ultimately, I ended up ghosting her (which is common), but it's recommended that you formally bring your therapy relationship to a close to transition out.

I returned to my therapist from four years prior, who had always shown consistency in her practice and genuine concern for my feedback. Remember that therapy is for you. Especially if you're paying for it, sis!

Therapy Is Just Another Relationship

You don't need to go through three months of sessions with the wrong therapist in hopes that it will work out or that their approach or behavior will change.

Treat this like any other relationship. If it feels wrong, or if there are some red flags, you can certainly exit stage left.

CHAPTER 3

Family and Friends Discount

BLOOD IS THICKER THAN WATER, BUT SO IS TOXIC WASTE

Blood Is Thicker than Water, But So Is Toxic Waste

Throughout your life you've probably heard the whole "blood is thicker than water" mantra.

It's bullshit. This idiom is spewed as a means to "keep families together," but it only does so by making the person suffering feel guilty and allowing others to escape accountability for toxic behavior. I'm here to tell you, if any member of your family is consistently bringing you harm, be it verbal or physical, you are well within your right to set up boundaries and distance yourself.

There have been times in my life where I ultimately decided it was best to sever ties with specific family members only to be guilted into reconnecting, and the same bullshit happened all over again.

Luckily, with the help of my therapist, I've reclaimed my peace and set boundaries. Yes, we're related, and no, I don't have to engage with you if you are continuing to bring havoc into my life.

Where It Counts

As a kid, I longed for the picture-perfect nuclear family I'd seen on TV and that some of my classmates seemed to have. When my life didn't mirror what I saw, I was embarrassed. I could only assume that something was wrong with me because I couldn't understand why I was undeserving of the care that kids were supposed to get from their parents.

My grandmother was the one who stood in to give me that unconditional love and support I always wanted. Every morning at 6 am, this 86-year-old woman would wake up to watch me walk to the bus stop. I will never forget the day a kid on my school bus yelled, "WHOSE GRANDMA IS THAT?" when they saw her standing in the middle of the street in her muumuu. I slinked my head down into my seat to hide my face. Looking back, although I was just a kid, I wish I had focused less on what I didn't have and more on how selflessly my grandmother looked after me. Family can simply be the ones who show up for you.

YOU CAN MUTE THE FAMILY GROUP CHAT

Forgiveness: Way Less Wavy than I Thought

Okay, I know this is a controversial take, but not everyone is entitled to your forgiveness. We are socialized to be the "bigger person" and turn the other cheek to those who've done us wrong. Giving someone the benefit of the doubt is emotionally expensive. I've found myself extending undeserved forgiveness to people who turn around and take advantage of it to get what they want, leaving me to labor and fix the damage they left yet again.

It's a scam and a set-up. Sure, there are instances when people genuinely hold themselves accountable for their own actions, and I see no harm in forgiving them and choosing to move forward in the way that best suits you. However, let's focus on the ones who don't.

I can't stress enough how much you need to be stingy when it comes to being so quick to forgive folks for your own well-being. Not everybody deserves your forgiveness. I'm going to say that again, in bold, so you can hear me:

Not everybody deserves your forgiveness.

Since we're here, let's be clear. Some shit *is* unforgivable. Only you can determine what that boundary is for yourself. Forgiving someone does not mean shit goes back to normal. You do not have to pick up where you left off in your relationship.

BEING THE BIGGER PERSON IS A SCAM

Your feelings are valid.
You don't need to give shitty behavior a pass.

DON'T FORCE YOURSELF TO FORGIVE

The Silent Treatment, aka The Road to Nowhere

I've notoriously used the silent treatment to demonstrate how I feel, and some of those times, my emotional intelligence was a bit undercooked.

I would assume the person on the receiving end could somehow read my mind and immediately understand what I was feeling—and rectify their behavior based on that. But receiving the silent treatment leaves most people confused. More often than not, people didn't understand that I was hurt until I had gone days without responding, leaving them trying to guess what triggered my distance.

The problem with the silent treatment is that it doesn't lead anywhere. Eventually, the person on the receiving end translates it as abandonment, and the relationship begins to deteriorate because they stop reaching out to see what's wrong. My best friend calls me out when I start acting like this, but it's not on her to perform that labor when I could just level up and articulate how I feel.

In hindsight, I wish I could've handled some of those friendships differently. The silent treatment contributed to the ultimate collapse of these relationships, and maybe being vulnerable enough to express how I felt would've been easier than masking my emotions with contempt. I'll do better.

YOU SHOULD

CALL THEM OUT ON THEIR BULLSHIT
CALL THEM OUT ON THEIR BULLSHIT
CALL THEM OUT ON THEIR BULLSHIT
CALL THEM OUT ON THEIR BULLSHIT
CALL THEM OUT ON THEIR BULLSHIT
CALL THEM OUT ON THEIR BULLSHIT
CALL THEM OUT ON THEIR BULLSHIT
CALL THEM OUT ON THEIR BULLSHIT
CALL THEM OUT ON THEIR BULLSHIT
CALL THEM OUT ON THEIR BULLSHIT
CALL THEM OUT ON THEIR BULLSHIT
CALL THEM OUT ON THEIR BULLSHIT
CALL THEM OUT ON THEIR BULLSHIT
CALL THEM OUT ON THEIR BULLSHIT
CALL THEM O

Back with the Bullshit
Sure, it's affirming to know I cut someone off for some fuck shit, but it's cathartic as all hell to let them know exactly how they had you fucked up.

Impact Matters More

Impact matters more than intent. How often have you heard "Sorry, that wasn't my intention" as a catchall response to someone who's been harmed? Sure, they may not have intended to hurt anyone, but it doesn't lessen the impact of the action. If someone accidentally slaps you, it still fuckin' hurts. Accountability includes not only acknowledgment of your actions but also an honest reflection of how those actions affect others.

Someone who vehemently dismisses how they made you feel, regardless of their intention, is showing you they don't care. In this case, move around. I promise you, they ain't really working on "changing." They are holding on to the idea that they can continue to count on you to overlook their bullshit. Continuous empty apologies that aren't followed by actionable steps to improve are nothing short of manipulation.

GRUDGES

RE JUST PERSONAL BOUNDARIES OTHER PEOPLE DON'T AGREE WITH

IT TAKES A LOT OF ENERGY TO MISMANAGE PEOPLE'S FEELINGS

Assumed Invitations

My grandma once said, "I don't go nowhere where I'm not wanted."

I learned about relationship deal breakers in therapy. A deal breaker is a hard boundary that can't be repaired if broken. Everyone has their own deal breakers. In partnerships, it could be cheating. With family, it could be disrespecting your decision to grow outside of their limited expectations. When it comes to friendship, my deal breaker is intentional exclusion.

If they're your "close friends" and they didn't personally invite you out, and they're freely posting their fun on Instagram without you, don't bother inserting yourself into the mix again.

It's the kind of passive-aggressive bullshit that I just can't overlook. Friends don't seek to intentionally hurt you.

Remember your feelings are valid. You don't have to justify them, ESPECIALLY to someone who has hurt you.

RELATIVELY

FRIENDLY

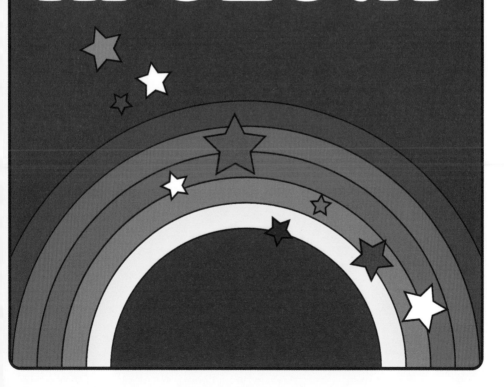

TIME PASSING IS NOT AN APOLOGY

BOUNDARIES WITHOUT ENFORCEMENT ARE JUST SUGGESTIONS

RUN THAT BACK

The Friend Breakup

We're all familiar with what a romantic breakup is. What many people don't talk about is the fact that an equivalent exists for friendships, and in some cases, it hurts so much more. I've had my share of friend breakups for various reasons:

- Roommates gone wrong (Don't move in with friends. Just don't.)
- Lack of trust emerged after an irreparable fall out
- Unequal amount of effort to maintain the friendship

It happens, and it sucks. Coming to terms with the fact that a supportive friendship that sustained well over several years can easily transition into nothing is a pain like no other. The photos in your phone of the good times you had together serve as painful reminders of something you can't return to. The tinge of discomfort and anxiety you feel in your stomach whenever you see them post on social media can be too much. Friendships ain't linear. It's common to take breaks. It's common to grow apart. There's no rule that says you have to maintain the same friendship forever. The friends you have growing up might not be your closest friends in adulthood.

There are going to be times when you wish things could return to what they were before, but ultimately you know it's just wishful thinking. Unlike the end of a romantic relationship, where you can instantly redirect your mindset to "there's plenty of fish in the sea," we don't think about that when it comes to friends because friendships are the relationships we deem irreplaceable. They're around before, during, and after romantic relationships. They keep us grounded. Walking away from that is a loss that invokes the five stages of grief:

1. **denial**
2. anger
3. **bargaining**
4. depression
5. **acceptance**

As I write this, I'm currently sitting somewhere between stages four and five, and I'm still in the process of learning to accept how things have become. I'm sad that a friendship is gone, and I'm learning to somehow appreciate that person for what they were at a particular time of my life. Are they inherently bad people? Not really. Did they do something that was incredibly hurtful to me? Yes. I've come to reckon with the fact that both can exist and our paths are just different now.

Do I wish them the best? LMFAO. No.

WHEEL OF CLOSURE

APOLOGY
DENIAL
SILENCE
ACKNOWLEDGMENT
CHANGED BEHAVIOR
CHANGED BEHAVIOR
ACKNOWLEDGMENT
SILENCE
DENIAL
APOLOGY

The Novelty of Closure
The closure you have is the closure you get. I truly believe that "closure" was a holiday created by greeting card companies. Don't wait on closure or apologies that may never come. All it does is occupy space and prolong the healing process.

CHAPTER 4

The Birds
&
The Birds

The Puzzle of Sexuality

The journeys to figuring out your sexuality and accepting it are two totally different paths.

In my case, by the time I was in the seventh grade, I knew. Consequently, I also knew I couldn't live these things out loud in my social circles.

Knowing that you're into women but being afraid to mention it to your straight high school best friends because you're afraid they'll think you want to get with them and then you'll lose your homegirls is a real thing. Homophobia, both internalized and external, was constantly fucking with me.

I remember watching the cult-classic film *But I'm a Cheerleader* and seeing my life. Like the main character, Megan (Natasha Lyonne), I was a cheerleader. I didn't aesthetically rock the boat outside of when I went through my emo/scene queen Panic! At The Disco phase. I was a seemingly hetero-ass bitch. I think I kept up this act all the way through my senior year of college. I was intent on keeping up the facade even if it meant I wasn't fully living my best life. Ugh.

According to a 2013 study done by the Pew Research Center, the average age most queer folks begin to feel they're not hetero is around twelve, with lesbians and bisexuals coming to this feeling around thirteen (makes sense it was the seventh grade for me).

The average age queer folks across the board actually tell another person about their sexual orientation is twenty. And some not at all.

Eventually, I was just like "fuck it" around the time of my twenty-first birthday. Also, I should note that I moved to California, so that helped.

I didn't hide it anymore. If someone asked, I wouldn't lie or suppress it. I would just say it matter-of-factly. The fear of losing friends was no longer there anymore. I found a circle of queer friends and others who were just altogether on the same wavelength as me. Honestly, the most freeing thing was changing my discovery settings on Tinder to also see women, instead of just a bunch of dudes, without the fear of being outed.

I also want to add, you don't need to have some huge public "coming out" debutante moment. Your queerness isn't any less valid. You aren't any less liberated. There's this unnecessary social pressure on queer folks to come out, as if queer identity is something to be publicly performed and for the consumption of others. It's for you, bb. You don't need any outside approval. You're not obligated to explain to friends, family, or strangers who you are. It ain't their damn business.

No one is expected to come out as straight because it's seen as the default and everything else must be explained for the comfort of the majority. Fuck that shit. Legitimately, do you.

Coming out is a privilege and not a requirement to legitimize queerness.

My Neck, My Back, My Clit?

I first learned how to masturbate in the seventh grade. I discovered my clitoris by sheer luck. But I can tell you right now, the moment I discovered that I could make myself cum, I was excited to catch the school bus home to do it again.

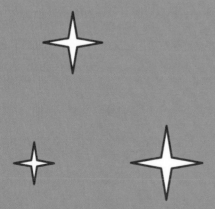

Bi, Bi, Bi

Freely embracing my sexuality was one of the best decisions I've made. However, it didn't come without the internalized pressure to openly perform and prove my queerness so as to feel that I wasn't some imposter taking up space. I spent so much of my high school and early college years cosplaying as straight that I felt I missed out on the experiences that I thought you needed to have in order to truly identify as queer.

I had only crushed on girls, but at that point I had never kissed or went out on any dates with other girls. I had only been in relationships with male partners. It was 2014 and I hadn't even watched seasons 1–4 of *The L Word* yet (I was a fan of the show's controversial reality series *The Real L Word* when it aired—yes, I know that doesn't count). When I finally had intimate relationships with women, I felt more like my actualized self. However, I try to divorce the idea that my experience of eating pussy validates my sexuality any more than my own existence. Eating pussy is a top-tier activity, tho!

The point is, like many of my bi homegirls, I struggled with validating my sexuality outside of queer relationships. It's almost if we're telling our brains, "How you feel is not enough! You need to be knee-deep in pussy at all times to identify as bi." And while yes, I love being knee-deep in pussy, I also

understand that the definition of bisexuality is an attraction to both the same and the opposite sex simultaneously. But, let's be real here. Biphobia exists. The expectation that bisexual folks can only exist in queer relationships is erasure. It also contributes to the idea that bisexuality is an identity that is only defined by who you are dating in that exact moment. I can 100 percent assure you my Kinsey test results will be the same no matter who I'm dating.

To put it in perspective, think of it like this: If you're not dating anyone at all, you're not any less queer. Queerness isn't the absence of anything. It's an expansion.

Trigger Warning:
Pleasure Ain't Predatory

As someone who identifies as bisexual, I'm more than familiar with being ambushed by couples seeking a unicorn for a threesome. Typically, it starts out okay as a one-on-one relationship between me and another girl. Later, I'm conveniently introduced to her boyfriend, who's open to "having fun." This can be a shitty tactic to lower your defenses and pressure your consent because of the nature of the relationship you've already built. Pleasure ain't predatory, and "no" doesn't mean "convince me." The responsibility is 1000 percent on people to not be predatory assholes, but I've had to learn that saying no when you feel uncomfortable isn't wrong. Advocate for your own comfort and safety before sparing others' feelings.

"NO"
does not mean
'Convince me"

Your ego

can't make me

CUM

Tales from the Clit

Remember that time when:

They told you, "Welp, I guess I can't make you cum today," stopped fingering you, and then asked what they could eat at your place for breakfast?

They were eating you out and blew their breath in your vagina?

They slapped your vagina like you were in a porn?

They told you they go down on girls by spelling the alphabet on their pussies?

Women Cum First

Although I knew how to make myself cum like the back of my hand, there was a disconnect with orgasms when it came to my solo act versus being with a sexual partner . . . specifically male partners.

As time went on and I entered the realm of engaging in sex with men, my orgasm or lack thereof was rarely seen as a cause for concern. Growing up, I wasn't exactly given positive talks about sexual agency; I was just expected to avoid pregnancy. Even though I knew EXACTLY what I needed to get myself off, I never brought it up to my male partners because:

1. I was afraid it would make them feel bad
2. I thought I would ruin the mood by "complicating" sex
3. I psyched myself into believing that this is just how sex is, unless I have a rarely experienced penetrative orgasm

Hell, I would even tell partners, "No, it's okay if I don't cum." Bitch, what?!

Your pleasure is just as important as your partners'. Do not shy away from letting them know what you like.

I used to be embarrassed about using a vibrator for clitoral stimulation during sex, thinking my partner would feel inadequate, even though I know it allows me to cum 100 percent of the time. (Well, except for that one time, but I eventually did. I was just super nervous and suffering from a little performance anxiety because I really liked this person.)

Practice letting your partner know that you'd like to introduce a toy during intercourse. For me, I usually just take a beat and say, "Hey, do you mind if I use my vibrator?" Most of the time, my partners have been down with it—even my large-ass Magic Wand.

Consequently, anyone that makes me feel bad for advocating for my own pleasure during sex is not someone I would share my body with long-term. Egos don't lead to orgasms.

Kink Possible

I first got into kink and BDSM in 2014. I initially tried and failed as a submissive with a partner. I learned I was not submissive at all, but dominant.

The first person I topped was someone I met on Tinder who was on tour with a band. They told me that every time their band came to LA, they visited various dominatrixes. At this time, I had been researching the lifestyle and was pretty geeked to try it out. We texted about it for maybe a week. We discussed hard limits (things you absolutely do not want to do) and soft limits (things you might not enjoy or prefer to enjoy with elevated caution), and then decided we would have a scene together.

I went to The Stockroom—a local kink-positive sex shop in LA—and purchased a riding crop. I decided that would be my implement of choice (and it was low-key all I could afford). They came over one afternoon, we went over the hard limits/soft limits again, how to address me during our scene, and I gave them a safe word. I left the room (I actually just went in my closet to change into heels and lingerie while I made them strip naked). I emerged like this trill-ass femme fatale butterfly out of the cocoon in complete Domme mode.

It was invigorating, and I honestly felt like a part of me was finally being fulfilled in a way that it never had before. Afterward,

they told me that I should consider doing this professionally . . .
Three years later I became a professional dominatrix.

AHT AHT!

I know, I know. The world of kink is awesome. However, it would
be irresponsible of me to not mention that your safety comes
first. A few tips:

- Consider making up a scene name for yourself (whatever
  you want). Don't give out personal information to
  strangers online, no matter how cool they seem.
- Look for sex-positive safe spaces. It's good to join
  communities and networks that prioritize the safety of its
  members.
- SSC (Safe, Sane, and Consensual): It's an acronym
  that's been in the kink community since the '80s.
  Basically, it means to safely gauge risks by making
  sure you're educated in whatever kink you're interested
  in, make decisions and engage in kink while in a clear
  headspace, and know you are in control. If you don't feel
  comfortable with something, DON'T DO IT! Additionally,
  no one should pressure or "convince" you to do anything
  you don't enthusiastically consent to.
- Whenever possible, try to bring a friend with you to play
  parties. If you can't for whatever reason, always let
  someone know where you are. Drop a pin so they know
  your location.
- Don't meet up with someone you met online by yourself.
  Always suggest meeting in public play spaces. If they are
  vehemently against that or pressure you to come to their
  home/hotel or some other space that could potentially
  inhibit your safety, decline and find someone else.

YES, THEY NEED TO TELL YOU IF THEY ARE SLEEPING WITH OTHER PEOPLE

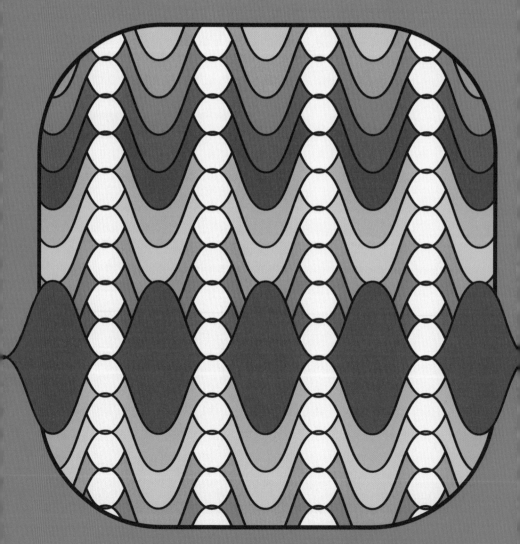

You + Me + Who Else?

Clearing this up once and for all: If your partner is lying to you (either outright or by omission) about sleeping with other people, it's a big red flag. The reason you might feel hurt or violated is because it's a violation. Full stop.

You deserve transparency no matter what stage of dating you're in.

You have a right to consent to sleeping with someone who has multiple partners and vice versa.

You are not tripping.

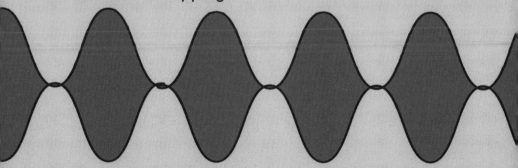

CHAPTER 5

So Y'all Talk

The Da

Meet new person

"Bonus Breadcrumbing"
or
they still watch your instagram story

Ghosted

"Things have just been super busy."
"I'm bad at texting."
Social media contradictions

Replies to texts and DMs
get slower

Hang out more
with zero clarity on
where things are going

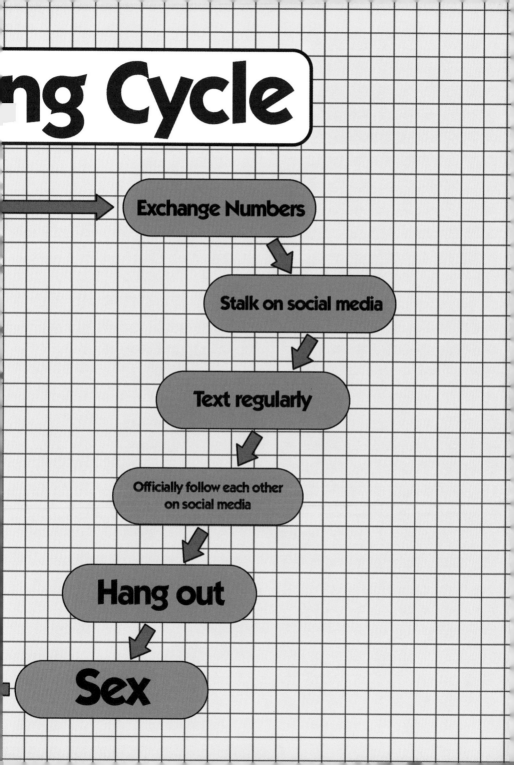

The Dating App Cycle

APRIL

You meet someone on a dating app. Let's say it's Tinder.

You talk every day, throughout the entire day. There's never a gap in how often you talk.

Are you getting the picture that you talk to them A LOT?

You finally agree to have your first date on Thursday. You prep and go back and forth with yourself over what to wear: Should you rock red lipstick? Will that deter you from making out later on in the date?

Soon, you find resolve for all of your pre-date issues.

You're ready. You head to the agreed-upon spot.

You're anxiously awaiting their arrival.

The first fifteen minutes go by and you naturally assume your date is running a little late because traffic, parking, etc. After all, you weren't exactly on time either.

Then thirty minutes goes by and there's no sign of your date.

You start to get a bit worried.

You send a "Hey, I'm sitting by the window" text. Nothing. Then two hours go by.

You log on to Twitter and see your potential date is retweeting Steve Lacy's album release with the flame emoji.

You go home.

You block.

JUNE

You meet someone on a dating app. Let's say it's Bumble. You talk every day, throughout the entire day. There's never a gap in how often you talk.

Are you getting the picture that you talk to them A LOT?

You finally agree to have your first date on Saturday.

You prep and go back and forth with yourself over what to wear: Should you wear your natural hair even though you bought this really cute wavy lace front unit that makes you feel like H.E.R.? Will you feel weird if y'all are hooking up later and you have to dodge so they don't dig their hands into your lace and feel your stocking cap-covered braids?

You find resolve for all of your pre-date issues.

You're ready.

You head to the agreed-upon spot.

You're anxiously awaiting their arrival.

They show up!

They're not what you expected.

You have been catfished.

You try to finish the date as politely as possible and then dismiss yourself to the bathroom to ask your friend to call you in ten minutes so you can fake an emergency and leave.

SEPTEMBER

You meet someone on a dating app! Let's say it's Hinge/ Raya/Feeld. You talk every day, throughout the entire day. There's never a gap in how often you talk. Okay, you know the drill here. You are envisioning hooking up with them while you play PARTYNEXTDOOR's "Thirsty."

You agree to have your first date on Friday. You prep, and this time you already know which outfit you're going to wear:

the leopard-print dress that you thrifted that shows off your favorite assets.

You beat your face and wear the red lipstick because why the fuck not?

You're ready.

You head to the agreed-upon spot.

You get there and they've texted you that they're sitting by the bar. You look up, and yes, their photos match how hot they are in person.

Y'all chat for a little bit and then you invite them back to your place.

You text a heads-up to your roommate, who's looking out for you since you previously told them you were meeting someone from a dating app, for safety reasons.

You're back at your place. You have sex. It's amazing.

You continue having sex for about six weeks, until . . . YOU CATCH FEELINGS.

You check in with your bae (who's not really your bae but just bae-adjacent) about your feels. They agree you should take things to the next level. You're excited.

Two days later, they call you to let you know they've changed their mind. Fuck.

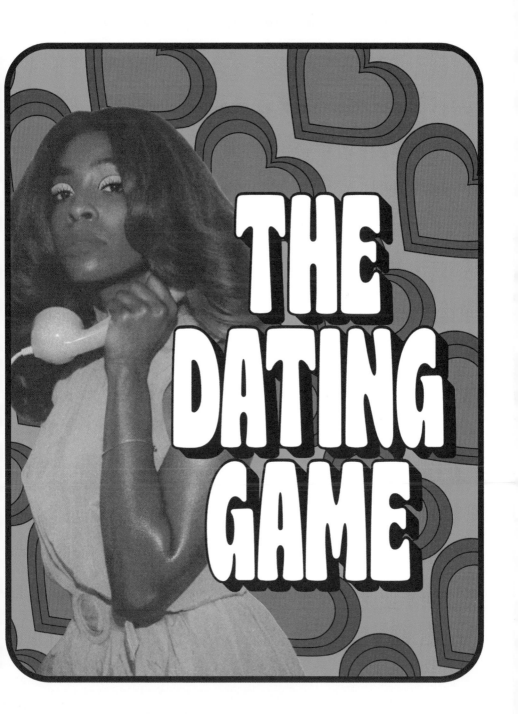

An Ex Is an Ex Is an Ex

When you break up with a partner or end a situationship, there's the unspoken "rule" that you must play into the nice girl narrative, no matter how shitty of a person they were to you. This is a plea for you to reject that bullshit.

Handle things in a way that is authentic to you. How you feel is 100 percent valid. You're not a politician campaigning for the vote of someone who ghosted you. You do not need to acknowledge their presence when they come around. You do not need to fake-ask them about their day when they couldn't bother to treat you with a teaspoon of respect.

And I don't care what anyone says, you don't need to be friends with your exes, ESPECIALLY immediately after a breakup. Why, sis?

AN EX IS AN EX

AN EX IS AN EX

AN EX IS AN EX

AN EX IS AN EX

IF YOU INITIALLY CURVE THEM BUT LATER GIVE THEM A CHANCE, THEY WILL WORK THE HARDEST TO WASTE YOUR TIME

You Curved Them for a Reason
Maybe you aren't physically attracted to them.
Maybe you aren't mentally attracted to them.
Maybe they don't have the qualities you know you need in a partnership.

If given the opportunity, they will surely waste your time as if they checked off every single thing on your list of needs.

SHOULD I DOUBLE TEXT THEM?

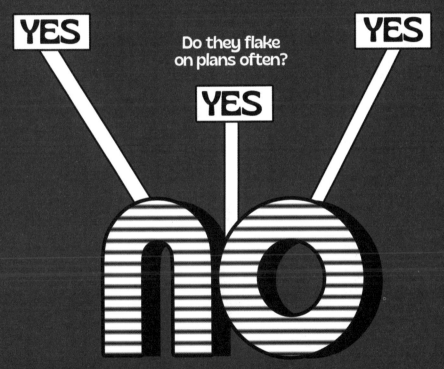

Are you always the first to reach out?

YES

Do they flake on plans often?

YES

Are they very active on social media?

YES

no

Sure, it's nice to get clarity, but if this person is conveniently "forgetting" about you or has all of a sudden gotten too busy to respond, it's best to move on. Ambiguity is a ne

POSTING SONG LYRICS ABOUT YOUR EX ON SOCIAL MEDIA IS GIVING THEM TOO MUCH ATTENTION

The Principle of Least Interest

In 1938, sociologist Willard Waller did a study on emotional availability between couples. It resulted in what we know as "The Principle of Least Interest," and it's something you've most likely been engaging in for years.

The Principle of Least Interest simply states that the person who cares the least about continuing a relationship has the most power in the relationship. Now, what does having less power look like IRL? Let me break this down.

A. When you have to question why the person you've been dating for over three months has been texting back more slowly or habitually "forgets" to reply.

B. If they're not making plans to see you. If you're planning all the dates and continuously asking them if they're free.

C. They're in no rush to discuss the relationship even though you've been dating and fucking for six months (more on this later in the chapter).

D. If they're consistently pulling disappearing acts for long periods of time. Are you dating fucking Carmen San Diego?

E. When you're constantly attempting to rationalize their otherwise irrational behavior by making excuses for them. Like, girl, sure, they could be sad about xyz, but they didn't tell YOU that, did they?

Now, after engaging in this trash-ass merry-go-round for years, where I was constantly in the position of least power (save a few individuals I didn't want to date anyway), I recognized that the best position to be in is the one in which I'm prioritizing myself. Yes, IG cuffed is cute every now and again, especially if you meet a cool-ass person. However, you know what really *is* fire? Minding my own shit.

That means:
- No overthinking the actions of someone else.
- Eliminating the worry of not being texted back. If that means you have to send a text message and put that phone on Do Not Disturb so anxiety doesn't peak (like me), do it.
- Eliminate time wasters. If they violate once, address it. If they violate again doing the same bullshit that you've already addressed, leave them on read.
- Listen to Meg the Stallion's *Tina Snow* album.

Do not allow any clown to treat you like you're not that bitch.

VULNERABILITY

SHARING FEELINGS DOESN'T MAKE YOU UNCOOL

Crimes against Vulnerability

Catching and expressing your feelings in this economy? Tuh.

Not-so-fun fact: I've historically avoided vulnerability.

The way my generation stigmatized liking someone and letting them know how you feel is one of the biggest crimes against modern courtship. Like, we really made it so that the emotions that naturally develop when dating are deemed a burden of pressure.

So I stuck to the norm of seeming too cool and disinterested in people I actually like for fear that my true display of emotions would make me seem like I'm some weak-ass bitch. (Yes, I know I need to work on my internal dialogue.)

The person you really like is then left to decode your feelings, and yeah, *that 100 percent always works out the way you want it to.* *eyeroll*

Look, I can admit I'm still a work in progress, but I can also tell you that expressing how you truly feel has benefits. You're able to see if the feeling is mutual instead of getting stuck in a cold war, wondering if the lyrics they posted on their Instagram story from "Say Something Loving" by The XX are about you.

90-DAY
RETURN POLICY

90-Day Return Policy*

I'm about to save you a lot of time with this one.

It does NOT take someone more than three months to decide if they want to be in a full-blown relationship with you.

Yes, that's right. If you've been hanging out with someone for over ninety days and they continue to act like the jury is still out or it's "too soon to talk about relationships," collect your things and return them to the streets.

*Does not apply to hookup-only situations, but be careful. Feelings can sneak up on you with a quickness when the sex is flames.

YES, I'M GONNA **LURK** BUT ONLY AFTER IT'S BEEN 6 MONTHS

Hurt Hunting

Lurking is hurt hunting.

You know you don't have a clear goal in mind, but you lurk until your feelings get hurt, and why would you want to put yourself through that, friend?

To eliminate any attempts at hurt hunting, you'll need to eliminate:

- lurking on their Instagram page from your burner account
- watching their Instagram stories from your friend's burner account
- soft stalking any person's account that leaves heart-eye emojis in their comments
- checking their tagged photos
- checking their close friends' tagged photos
- watching the Instagram stories of their family members
- "accidentally" showing up at the place you know they hang out at, hoping to run into them
- watching their social media to see if you can attend an event they've been mentioning going to (this also borders on actual stalking—DON'T do this!)
- attempting to get really close with their friends post-breakup; their friends are up on game, and it's weird

CERTIFICATE OF

PRESENTED TO

_____

FOR GOING OUT OF YOUR WAY TO
RUN INTO THE PERSON THAT GHOSTED YOU

ON THIS DAY _____ OF YEAR _____

YOUR WORTH ISN'T DETERMINED BY YOUR RELATIONSHIP STATUS

For What It's Worth

Your value is not determined by whether or not your phone is dry. Being single is valid. This is not a book that is going to stan heteronormative relationship culture. You know the ones that essentially make you hyperfocus on, eat, sleep, and breathe the pursuit of a relationship? I've read those books. They suck.

Being attached to another human doesn't outshine everything you've ever done. It's okay to desire partnership, but it's also okay to not desire it.

Slow Fading, Ghosting, Orbiting, and Breadcrumbing

Once upon a time, long ago, there was an old fairy tale that said that after you stopped dating someone, you wouldn't have to see them live out their lives for the rest of eternity. That was the world before social media.

Today, the dating cycle not only includes a cease in contact but an incredibly unhealthy amount of lurking from yourself or the other party.

So you've reached one of the final stages of the dating cycle. Let's take a moment to quickly review how this can play out:

Slow fade: Where the responses get sparse and the other party all of sudden gets "too busy" to hang out. "Things have been so busy" works because it:

    a) Allows them to have a legitimate reason for their change in behavior

    b) Makes it so you can't question the behavior without seeming irrational

This can also also look like them being extremely active online but intentionally choosing not to engage with you or your posts. If you bring it up, they might say something along the lines of "social media isn't real" or "I don't take social media seriously," when in actuality social media is the #1 way a lot of us engage with our friends and lovers on a daily basis. Someone's social media habits can absolutely be representative of how they feel in real life. Think about it. The first thing so many folks do after falling out with someone is passive-aggressively mute their Instagram posts and stories instead of directly resolving the issue at hand. Slow fading allows the exiting party to escape the responsibility of bringing things to a formal close and leaves the remaining party feeling a bit gaslighted if they choose to bring up how those actions are affecting them.

Ghosting: Self-explanatory. This is a no-call, no-show. They disappear into thin air after leaving you on read or blowing off a date. Don't expect to hear from them again unless . . .

Orbiting: Ghosting with a twist. They've left you on read, but they still watch your Instagram story. This means nothing. They want you to know they're still around but ultimately don't want to engage with you any further. But sometimes you do hear from them and . . .

Breadcrumbing: They're orbiting you, and ultimately they're waiting for an opportunity to toss out some half-ass Instagram like or noncommittal interaction to ensure they still have access to you. Don't mistake this for anything other than the fact that they feel like you're probably about to move on and they need to make sure they can still wedge themselves into the mix.

Read Receipts

If their response time is getting noticeably slower, to the point where they are barely responding at all but are still posting on social media . . . they don't fuck with you like that, and that should be your cue to move around.

Again, don't make excuses for them. Don't let them "My bad! I'm gonna do better" you to death. You've reached the end of this courtship/situationship. If they're not respecting your time, they're not respecting you. They will do it again and again because they feel they can get over on you since you've accepted that behavior before without consequence.

Exhibit I

Wednesday, 3:45 pm

  Them: Hey, hope you've been good.

Wednesday, 3:50 pm

  You: Hey, you! It's been hectic. A lot of work to get done before this event on Saturday. How are things going for you?

FOUR DAYS LATER

Sunday, 1:45 pm

  Them: I've been good. I hope your event was dope.

This is lackluster. They are intentionally not applying pressure. This is what a slow fade looks like. It's best to just leave them on read.

INSTAGRAM STORY STOP CHECKING TO SEE IF THEY WATCHED YOUR INSTAGRAM STORY STOP CHECKING TO SEE IF THEY WATCHED YOUR INSTAGRAM STORY STOP CHECKING TO SEE IF THEY WATCHED YOUR INSTAGRAM STORY STOP CHECKING TO SEE IF THEY WATCHED YOUR INSTAGRAM STORY STOP CHECKING TO SEE IF THEY WATCHED YOUR INSTAGRAM STORY STOP CHECKING TO SEE IF THEY WATCHED YOUR INSTAGRAM STORY STOP CHECKING TO SEE IF THEY WATCHED

COMPROMISING YOUR NEEDS AIN'T CUTE

Chameleon Couture

I can't stress the importance of this enough: Do NOT change your personal goals, values, and desires to match a partner. There are billions of people on this planet, and I promise that you won't have to become someone else to find your person.

In the past, I made the mistake of trying to shrink myself to fit into the life of a partner, and it stifled me. I put too much of my energy into making sure that I was everything my partner desired, and I found myself shamefully attempting to meet the standards they set with previous partners instead of recognizing the privilege it was to be with me. I allowed their constant comparisons to pressure me into being someone I never wanted to be. (Stay away from narcissists, y'all.)

Most people who know me personally can attest that I'm very much a "this is what you get with me" type of bitch, so to get caught up in that cycle was embarrassing. I was a shell of myself, with my self-esteem at its lowest. One of the major benefits of finally ending that relationship was that I could firmly stand in what I wanted and refuse to compromise.

If you envision your life being childfree, married, or fulfilled by a career, you don't have to negotiate. There's someone out there who will be 100 percent down for whatever you want. Don't settle. Don't change.

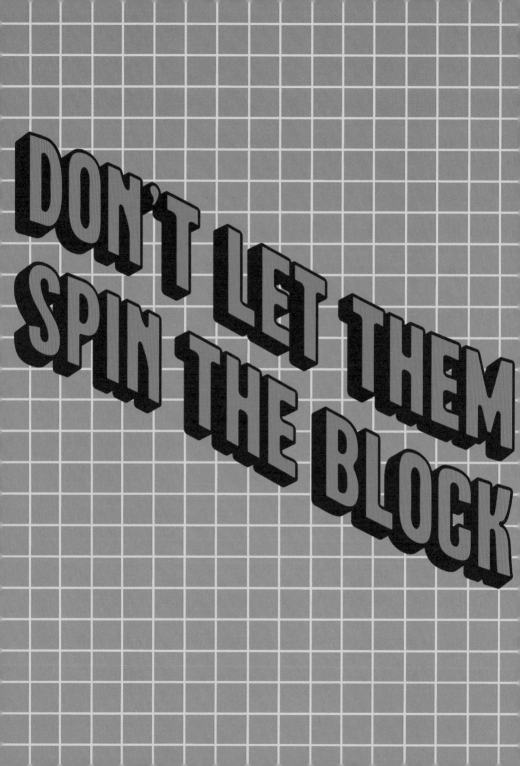

Don't Let Them Spin the Block

Don't let them spin the block. They do not get to pick you up and put you down at their convenience. You're a whole-ass human, babe.

"I'm not looking for anything, but I like hanging out with you."

Translation: I don't want to seriously date you, but I don't want to completely close the door on fucking you.

Have you or a loved one been told the above? You may be entitled to financial compensation.

The moment you hear these words from someone you're dating, you should start crafting your escape plan. It's the weakest bit of transparency available, but it's enough for you to get the fuck out of dodge.

This is not an invitation to keep dating to "see how things go" in hopes that the other party will eventually want a relationship with you. Nine times out of ten, they have already made up their mind about pursuing a serious relationship with you. If someone comes along that they really like, they WILL be "looking to get into a relationship" with them.

Don't let these words stall you. You will get your feelings hurt.

YOU ABOUT TO
GET YOUR
FEELINGS
HURT

Stop Making Excuses for the People You Date

Accept what they're giving you at face value.

I know we're socialized to be sympathetic and freely give out emotional labor, but shitty people know this and they will take advantage of it.

Sure, we all go through things in life. However, you are NOT their therapist. It is not your job to sit around and decode why they haven't opened up to you, or why they disappear for days or even weeks at a time while sometimes still posting on Instagram or watching your stories.

Making excuses for them sounds like:

"Maybe they're having a hard time at work."

"Well, I have issues too. So it could be me overthinking."

"Well, their cousin did get the flu, and I think they were maybe kinda close."

"Well, they're on tour, and I know being on the road is stressful."

"They've been filming skate videos all week, so they're probably just tired."

"They didn't sell as much of their art at their gallery show, so they're really sad."

"They just ran into their ex, and they need time to process."
"They just broke up with their ex, so that's why they pull
away from me sometimes."

RED FLAG WARNING: If you start telling yourself the last
two, please PLEASE leave. When an ex is still involved,
you are setting yourself up for some uncomfortable
truths. You soon realize you've become the rebound.
You assume the role of the "clean-up woman" á la the
late, great Betty Wright, and you take on the thankless
task of healing them back to emotional availability so
they can move on to the next relationship.

DON'T MISTAKE
SHORT-TERM
ATTENTION
FOR A
LONG-TERM
RELATIONSHIP

CHAPTER 6

On the Clock

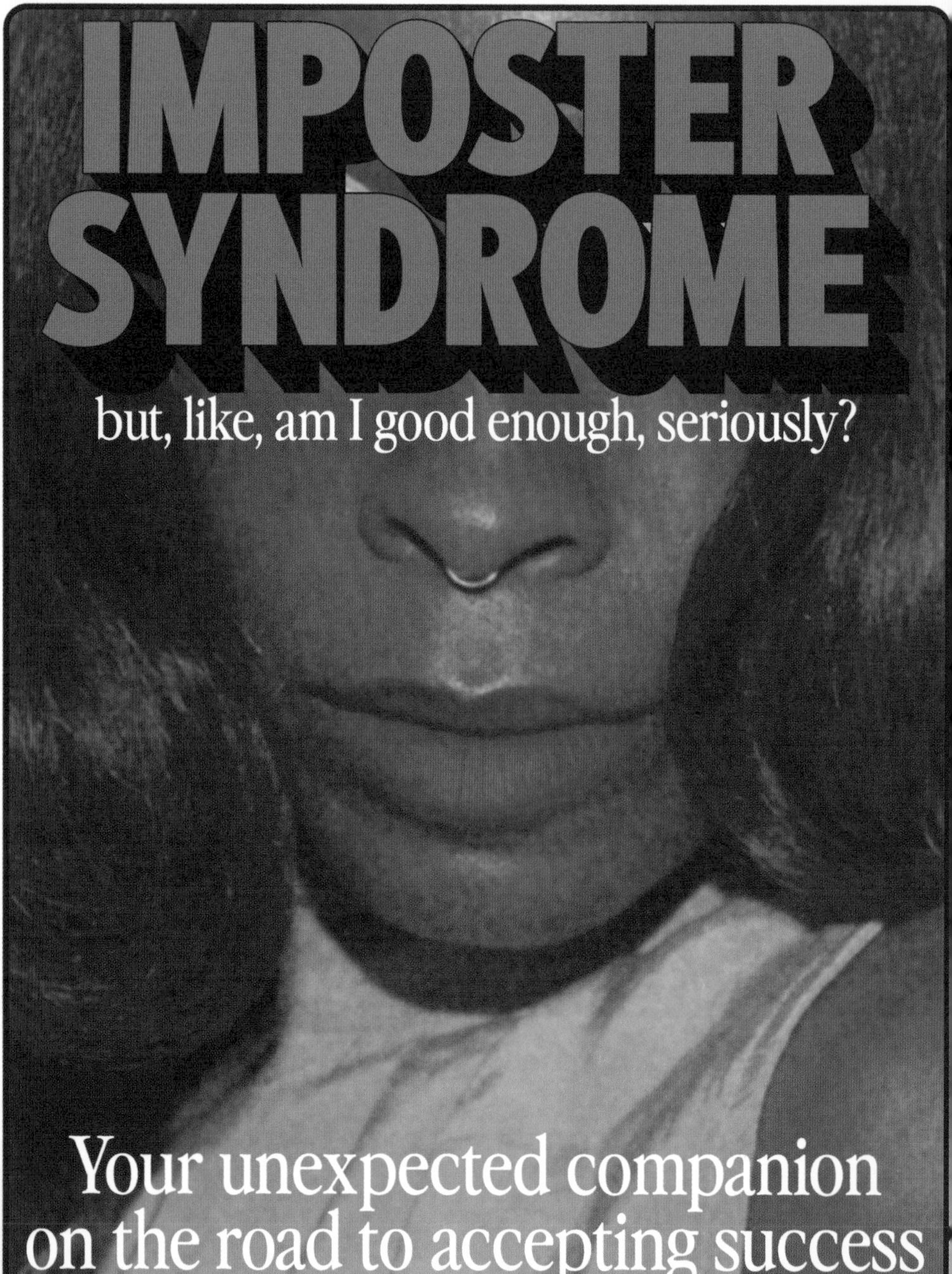
IMPOSTER SYNDROME
but, like, am I good enough, seriously?
Your unexpected companion on the road to accepting success

Imposter Syndrome

Imposter syndrome is a feeling of inadequacy stemmed from low self-confidence in your work.

How it shows up for me: I can't believe I am writing this book right now.

How it shows up for Pulitzer Prize, Tony Award, and five-time Grammy Award–winning writer and poet Maya Angelou: "I've written eleven books, but each time I think 'Uh oh, they're going to find out now. I've run a game on everybody and they're going to find me out."

Much like anxiety and depression, imposter syndrome does not discriminate. It doesn't matter if you're famous, successful, wealthy, and have visibly "made it," it will make its presence known.

How to push back on these feelings of inadequacy in two steps (I'm still working on this myself):

Focus on the work you've done to get to where you are. It's easy to feel like you're an imposter when you can't remember the steps that got you into the room.

Ignore perfection. Please. I am a Virgo rising, big 'ol perfectionist, and it's that same perfectionism that keeps me from seeing the good in my work. Repeat until you get out of your head. I promise you deserve to be there, unless you are a scammer for real, and in that case . . . I got nothin'.

You can say NO

without explaining yourself

Waiting to Excel

Prioritize your well-being at work.

That means: Take your lunch—even if you're the only person on the job taking an outside lunch, take it. Just because your job tries to socialize you to work through lunch doesn't mean you should. Even if you bring your lunch, take it outside.

Ideally, you should:

Get some fresh air.

Block out the bullshit for thirty minutes, or an hour if you're lucky.

Put on your headphones and watch a show on your phone to take your mind off work.

Plot how you're going to get out of this job if you hate it (actually use their time for this).

Plot how you're going to get ahead in this job if you see a future there.

Pull out your tarot deck.

Reread that text your date sent you that gives you butterflies.

Gone Head and Quit

Around 2013 I started working as a senior editor, and things were going alright for the first couple years. I worked from home, and it allowed me to go to auditions every now and again. My boss was cool. I considered her somewhat of a friend. However, that lasted all but a minute.

Out of the blue, in February 2015, this happened:
February 8th: I'm fired.
February 15: I'm hired back
February 20: I'm fired for the second time
February 24: I'm hired again

I was caught off guard both times I was let go because it felt like one day my boss woke up and decided I was expendable. It was chaos. As someone who's been diagnosed with generalized anxiety disorder, the stress of losing financial security twice in one month, let alone two weeks, was unbearable. After that, I felt completely unstable at work. I couldn't sleep, and when I did, I woke up almost every day thinking I would be spontaneously fired. This went on for months.

Around July, my boss and I were having a pleasant conversation about the job, and I received praise from her. She told me that I wouldn't have to worry about being fired again and that she was working on getting me health insurance.

The very next day, I received an email from her stating that she saw no value in me.

I was the one who facilitated much of the day-to-day supervision between writers and the editorial calendar, in addition to establishing a solid project management system overall. My entire financial well-being was tethered to someone's mood.

I quit. I would rather leave of my own accord and pursue a healthy work environment than risk having the rug pulled out from under me yet again.

Yes, it was a strain to walk away. My money was shorter than dudes who say they're 5'10" on dating apps (we know you're not 5'10", my guy). However, leaving an unsteady work environment for my mental health was worth it.

YOUR BOSS AIN'T YOUR FRIEND

But Did You Get My Invoice . . . ?

I have had the luck and sometimes misfortune of being a freelancer most of my adulthood. Sure, you don't necessarily have to work in an office. Your friends always assume you're free to hang out (you're not). You don't necessarily have an overbearing boss watching your every move. Sometimes you can make your own hours, even though most of us overwork ourselves.

HOWEVER. When it comes to money, it's legitimately the wild, wild west. I promise some of your favorite companies have probably stiffed a freelancer or paid them far beyond net thirty . . . I'm talking six months out. It seems like 90 percent of freelancing is chasing unpaid invoices.

So as a freelancer, treat clients the same way any other company would treat them:

- Provide your own contract upfront, outlining your own terms and conditions.
- Charge late fees or penalties if your terms are not met.
- Invoice through software that can track whether or not someone has viewed your statements. We all know accounting likes to play the whole "I never received your invoice" game to prolong issuing payments.
- Get a name and direct email from someone in the accounting department. That's one less barrier to your funds.

Ease On Down the Road:
How I Got Here

After I quit my editorial job in 2016, I took my very last check and paid the remainder of my rent for the year. At the time, I was paying a little under $700/month. I moved to LA on my own, and I was in constant fear of losing my housing, because I had absolutely nothing to fall back on, so I felt securing that was top priority.

I took a job as a Pro-Domme in a dungeon the following year because it allowed me the flexibility to still audition and it was something I already had some experience with. I continued to submit my writing to other media outlets in hopes that I would be commissioned for work.

A certain hip media outlet published a piece I was really proud of, while neglecting to tell me they didn't pay their contributors. I requested to remove the piece immediately, and then I then decided to self-publish it as a zine called *The Dudes You Date; The Vans They Wear.*

After publishing, I shared on social media that it was for sale in my online shop. It sold out and kept selling out. I never imagined my writing would connect with so many people. After all, I tweet almost daily into oblivion and nobody really pays attention.

Over the next year, I started booking more acting work

(TV + commercials), which allowed me to stop working as a Domme and devote more time to growing my little shop into what is now known as Brownie Points (for you). I then started selling the artwork I posted online as prints, and I later expanded into jewelry, shirts, and candles. I kept investing the money I earned back into the shop to develop more products, and I kept stumbling in the dark when it came to different aspects of running a business. I didn't have any mentors to turn to. It was just me, myself, and my Google searches.

I was running the entire operation all by myself (designing, producing, ordering, marketing, accounting), in addition to my regular design work, until June 2020, when people suddenly seemed to realize that Black-owned businesses existed. I was hit with so many orders that I couldn't keep up. Fast-forward to present day, when things have calmed down and I'm able to have support from someone whom I hired to help me full-time.

While I still feel I'm not as proficient in running a business as I would like, I'm constantly learning and in a way better position to keep up than I was even a few months ago.

NO DAYS OFF IS NOT A FLEX

YOU NEED REST, BABE

No Days Off Is NOT a Flex

There's something to be said about the prominence of "rise and grind" culture in our everyday lives. We live in a world that values productivity over personhood. You're pressured into neglecting the idea of rest to prove your worth.

I'm letting you know right now: YOU NEED REST, BABE.

The work will be there when you get back. One of the biggest lessons I had to learn was that my self-worth is not attached to visible output. Unfortunately, with social media, visibility becomes currency. You psych yourself into believing that there's no honor in rest and no virtue in putting out something deemed imperfect. You're then left both mentally and physically drained.

I can't even count the amount of times I've sacrificed my sleep for work. There were so many nights where I stayed up until 6 am instead of stopping at midnight and relieving myself to do the work in the morning. Spoiler alert: The work was still there the next morning.

As someone who spent their teenage years working two jobs and adulthood working up to three jobs to make ends meet, I understand there are times when you just can't even imagine being able to take a break. But prioritizing breaks leads to better overall quality of life. Even if it's a few minutes, take a step back and recognize when you're at your limit.

IS IT OKAY TO QUIT MY JOB?

Do any of the following apply?

- [ ] My valid concerns are dismissed
- [ ] It's affecting my mental health
- [ ] No one advocates for me
- [ ] I am being underpaid and overworked
- [ ] It's frowned upon to use sick days/personal days
- [ ] It's frowned upon to use vacation time
- [ ] I don't feel safe

Note: There is no minimum number of reasons

I AM ABSOLUTELY

DO:NE

FIGHTING BURNOUT

Things You're Not Supposed to Do That Will Get You Ahead

If you think I'm going to sit here and preach righteousness when it comes to applying for these jobs, you're wrong. Look, I want you to get ahead. And one of the things I've learned is that nepotism and proximity to straight, white male culture gives the privileged access to opportunity. So what's the next best thing for the rest of us? EMBELLISHMENT.

Lie on your resume

You learn how to do most jobs on the job anyway. Even if you possess a specific skill, every company has their own system they're going to want you to learn and adapt to. Just be willing to learn or at least bookmark a few videos of the skills that you've "embellished" on your resume. (Please note: Do not lie to get a job that requires specific life-saving skills—e.g., lifeguard if you don't know how to swim, or paramedic if you don't know CPR, etc.)

Use friends as references

I've definitely helped friends get jobs by pretending to be a coworker, supervisor, etc., and the same has been done for me in certain instances. The way I see it, if Tanner in the marketing department can get his cousin hired to run the company's social media accounts on the strength of just being his relative, what harm is it if your friend helps you?

Talk about your pay on the job

Companies literally bank on exploiting employees by implementing a culture of secrecy. This reinforces the increasing wage gap as it widens to the distance between Mars and the sun. You should absolutely know if you're being underpaid and then go leverage that to move on up, baby. There's nothing "unprofessional" about not wanting to be exploited.

CHAPTER 7

Money Can't Buy Happiness but It Can Pay My Rent

How I Lost Money, Part 1

I was sixteen years old, and I'd been working all summer to save up and pay for driver's ed and cheerleading costs at school. I would cash my checks and sometimes keep the money on me because I didn't have a bank account. I had around $280 on me that day.

So I'm getting my nails done in Houston at a random nail salon that I'd never been to before in the part of Third Ward we call "The bottoms." Two random dudes come in, encouraging everyone to play this game with one of them for money. The object of the game was to find the eraser hidden underneath three soda bottle caps, which he shuffled around.

I was geeked at the opportunity to win money and knew my skills were sharp AF, so I decided to try my luck. The first couple of times, I won (he let me win) a couple of $20 bills. Then, as I played a few more times, I noticed I kept losing horribly. The other adults in the salon were cheering me on to keep playing. One dude waiting in the salon even came up and tried his luck, only to lose $100. (Looking back on it, I think this guy was a plant.)

The final nail in the coffin was when this scammin'-ass dude proposed that I could play one last time to win the entire stack of money that he had in his hand if I put my last $20 up. There had to be over $800 or so in his hand. It was a lot.

I was confident that I could watch this man's hands effectively and there was no way I could lose. So I agreed to one final play. I just knew I was going to walk away with all that money, but then . . .

The heartbreak when the eraser wasn't under the soda bottle cap. This man jetted out the nail salon with all my money so fast. The dude who "lost" $100 went after him outside, but I think it was just to get his planted money back.

I started crying. I only had enough to pay for my $16 manicure plus tip, but half the money I needed to pay for driver's ed was gone. I called my folks, who showed up at the nail salon only to have virtually all of the adults there lie to their face and say, "We tried to tell her to stop." I was raised not to "talk back" to adults, so I just cried. Whew, I'm still hot over that.

As it turns out, I was a victim of what's known as a "pigeon drop." Two people will work together to scam you out of money by proposing you can make a larger sum if you just put up a certain amount.

I watched the 1992 Wayans film *Mo' Money* for the first time recently and was instantly triggered when I saw Seymour (Marlon Wayans) starting to pigeon drop with a game of "three card." Amber (Stacey Dash), walks over to play. However, unlike me, she ends up winning her money back because Johnny (Damon Wayans) is trying to cuff her.

FRIENDS
PAY YOU BACK

Personally, I Can't Loan to You

I gave an ex $40 in high school to pay his Sprint phone bill. He never paid me back, but kept flaunting how many stacks he had on Facebook. Real clown-girl shit.

Don't lend any money that you don't want to lose. I would go so far as to say don't lend any money. Unless you're an angel investor, keep your coins.

Don't flirt with me unless
you plan on paying off my

Student Loans

Student Loans

Senior year of high school, my cheerleading coach told me I wouldn't go to college, but look at me now, bitch! I got five figures in student loan debt!

In my opinion, in the grand scheme of things, student loan debt is at the bottom of my list of priorities. I've seen multiple viral stories of folks paying off six-figure student loans in a year, and they either:

1. Have a family with disposable income to help them pay it down
2. Take on a gazillion jobs without any time for rest in between

I don't have #1. I feel like #2 is just robbing you of living life. Sallie Mae and 'nem don't deserve that much effort as predatory as they are with these compounding interest rates. Sure, it's a high debt balance on your credit, but it is in fact possible to still go about your life and have good credit with a student loan balance. Ask for income-based repayment plans and keep it pushing.

DO NOT PAY SOMEONE TO MAKE MONEY

No Business like Scam Business

If someone is coming to you with a "business opportunity" that will turn you into a millionaire in thirty days but it's contingent on a hefty fee and how many people you can recruit by telling them the exact same thing, run.

If someone tells you that you can make $6000 by investing $500 in their "money loom/blessing circle," run.

I Am Financially Embarrassed

I first heard of the phrase "I'm financially embarrassed" in the 1973 Blaxploitation film *Cleopatra Jones*, and from then on I've thought it was the fanciest way to say "I'm broke."

There's been this taboo around money since I can remember. It's considered inappropriate to talk about. Heaven forbid someone thinks you are pocket watching.

Because I grew up not talking about money outside of asking my grandma for lunch money or for the Scholastic book fair, I was honestly real clueless when it came to managing my finances in adulthood.

Bad decisions that could've been avoided if I was exposed to conversations about money:

- student loans
- bad car deals
- credit card debt (why did I even need a credit card from a mall store?)
- pawn shops (related: NEVER do a payday loan or title loan!)
- overdraft fees (I probably raked up a few thousand)
- overplucked/threaded eyebrows

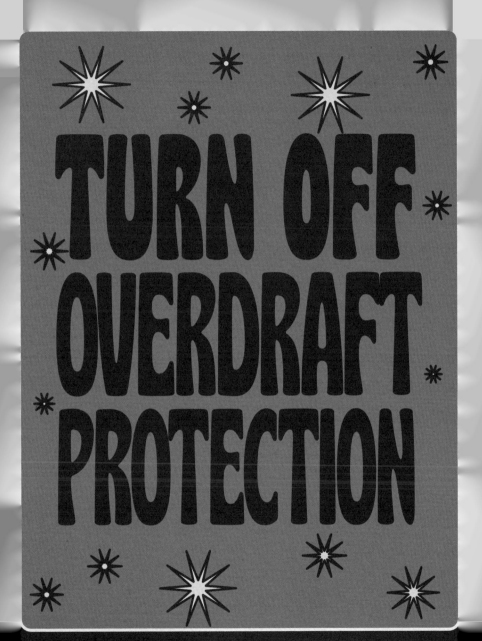

TURN OFF OVERDRAFT PROTECTION

Negative Balance

If I ain't got the money, I don't need the bank giving me a high interest loan I didn't ask for in the first place. Getting charged $35 for a $10 burger and fries is a scammmmmmmm.

NOT CHECKING YOUR BANK ACCOUNT DOESN'T MEAN THE MONEY WON'T LEAVE YOUR ACCOUNT

The Secret to Maintaining Your Bag . . .

is checking your account balance. I know, I know. It seems like the most mundane thing to do, but as someone who once racked up $1600 in overdraft fees, I can tell you right now: I have not been charged one of those little $35 money sucks since I turned off overdraft protection. Look for banks that won't charge you overdraft fees. They're bullshit. Think of keeping your money like growing your hair. You can't just put it up in a protective style and forget about it. You gotta check in, make sure it's moisturized, notice if there's breakage, and trim when necessary.

Now, you don't have to always log in to your account to do so. A while ago, I started using an online bank that immediately sent me a notification after I bought anything. There's something about not having to log in to my actual account to see my balance that seemingly took the pressure off. It was a small baby step toward financial responsibility.

Most recently, I upgraded to a budgeting app. Every week (almost . . . okay probably every other month, if I remember), I sit down and categorize my transactions. Yes, it's embarrassing to realize how much I spend on fast food. When I discovered zeppoles at Olive Garden, it was a problem. The Qdoba queso and random ICEEs from the gas station really add up. Seeing each of these transactions amount to more than what I would spend on monthly groceries puts the fear in my heart to chill out (even if it's just temporarily, because lord knows I'm tryin', but why did he create food trucks, tho?)

The bad-bitch level after this point is getting a solid financial advisor. Yes, a financial advisor is going to hold you accountable and help guide you to save for your future. Future savings can help with:

- retirement
- education
- investments
- TELFAR bag
- trip to Tulum

Be careful. There's still folks out there who will try to take advantage of you. Don't trust credit cleaning companies. You can fix your credit yourself. I lost $300 to a company who said they would fix my credit but left my credit score for dead.

While we're here:

If you freelance or work for yourself, paying quarterly taxes will save you a lot of headaches come tax time. Nobody likes paying several racks that feel like they came out of nowhere.

MONEY TALKS, AND YOU NEED TO SPEAK UP

CHAPTER 8

Words to Live By

Ignore
Perfection

Nothing Beat a Failure
But a Try

In the 1930s, my grandma moved to Texas by herself at fourteen years old. She was able to save enough money by working as a private duty nurse for a white family to move her parents and brother to Houston. She would later own restaurants and nightclubs in Houston's Third Ward throughout the 1950s in the segregated South.

"Nothing beat a failure but a try," is something I heard my grandma say often whenever she wanted to go for something without knowing how things would turn out. It's this exact quote that gave me the motivation to move to LA on my own.

We fixate a lot on waiting for the "right time" to pursue a lot of what we want in life, but this hypothetical perfect date doesn't truly exist. Sure, I could've saved three months' worth of expenses before moving to LA to afford more than a couple 50-cent tacos from Del Taco. But as an anxious procrastinator, I didn't have the discipline for that. It was a whole "now or never," and I had to leap and wait for the net to appear.

Years later, my grandma's words (and addressing my generalized anxiety disorder in a clinical setting) helped me confront my fear of failure. I've learned that it's better to have made an attempt at something than to go through life without knowing what could've been had you just tried.

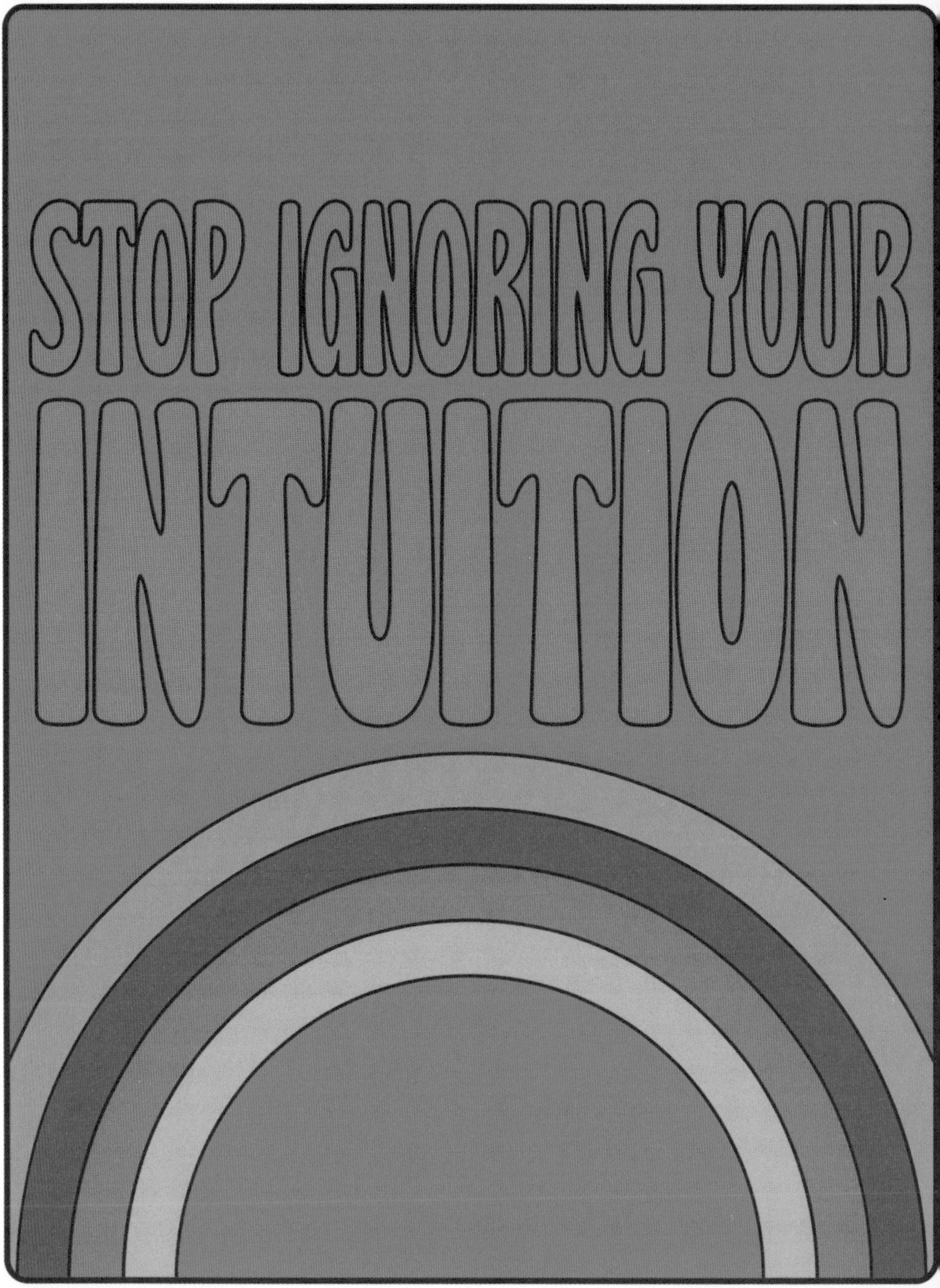
STOP IGNORING YOUR
INTUITION

LEAVE THEM ON READ

STOP GIVING PEOPLE THE BENEFIT OF THE DOUBT

IT'S EMOTIONALLY EXPENSIVE

SAVE YOUR ENERGY

You can save both your energy and dignity by not texting a paragraph to someone who doesn't even care if they hurt you

NOT EVERYONE IS GOING TO LIKE YOU

Not Everyone
Is Going to Like You

The truth is, you're not going to be the "good guy" in everyone's life story. And no matter how hard you try to appeal to everyone, you can't control whether or not they will like you. This doesn't mean go off and be an asshole, but it does mean you should free yourself from the burden of people pleasing. Stop doing labor for something you can't control.

I often find myself criticizing the work that I create so much that I constantly stall projects, this book included. Somehow, this idea of tearing myself down before anyone else had the chance to became a way of self-preservation for me. But I've realized you can't go through life trying to escape critique or differing opinions. It's impossible. All you're really doing is tripping yourself up.

Acknowledgments/Shout-Outs

If you've made it this far, congratulations! I wouldn't have without so many amazing people in my life. First and foremost: my late grandma, Helen aka Big Mama aka Meme. Even though you're not here in the physical, I am so grateful that being around you helped shaped me into the independent, bad bitch I never thought I was going to be. I know you're proud of me and always have my back. I miss you! Also, shout-out to my amazing aunt Sandra. I love you so much! You're one of the kindest, sweetest people, and you never hesitated to make sure I felt loved and cared for. I'm so lucky and proud to call you my aunt. Shout-out to my parents: I know I wouldn't be here without you. While the past is far from perfect, I appreciate the efforts y'all have continued to make to show up for me. Much love to the rest of my family in Texas. I love y'all! (Most of y'all.)

Shout-out to my friends who supported me to get this book done, especially through the shit show that was Summer 2020! Cecily (Coco), Lauren, Joy, Biniam, Cheeno, Sama'an, Stephanie, and my amazing assistant, Mariah: Y'all let me know you believed I could do it, even at times where I felt completely overwhelmed, and it helped push me through!

Shout-out to my therapist since 2016 and to my meds! Shout-out to Kevin Parker and his gift to the world that is Tame Impala.

Shout-out to the amazing Black creatives that helped me bring the cover to life: my photographer, Mahaneela, who had me looking radiant and the designer of my dream custom rhinestone cowgirl jumpsuit, Johnique of The Creatures!

Shout-out to everyone at Kokila and Penguin Random House! Sydnee and Jasmin, thank y'all so much for making my dream book come to life and extending me grace and the opportunity to share my voice with the world. And to my lovely lit agent, Monica, with Odom Media Management, for being so incredibly supportive. You really helped me do the unthinkable, which sometimes meant trusting myself. Shout-out to my managers, Matt and Anthony, at Principal Talent.

Shout-out to my hometown of Houston, Texas, and most importantly the Third Ward. Literally, everything I am is owed to my hood. I wouldn't want to be from anywhere else.

To my alma mater: Maybe if you forgave my student loans, I would have something nice to say.

Last but most certainly not least, all of y'all! No matter how you found me or where, I'm so grateful y'all have made me feel seen in so many ways.

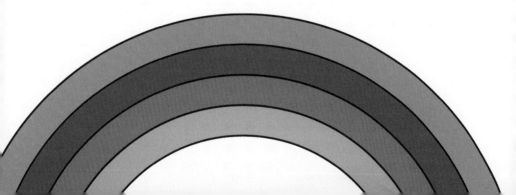